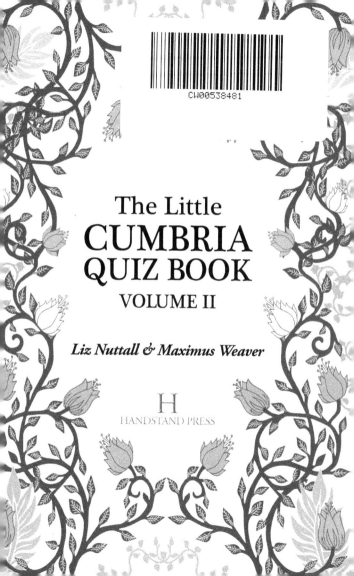

The Little
CUMBRIA
QUIZ BOOK
VOLUME II

Liz Nuttall & Maximus Weaver

H
HANDSTAND PRESS

Published by Handstand Press
Ulverston Cumbria.

www.handstandpress.net

First Published in 2021

ISBN: 9780957660991

Designed and set by Russell Holden
www.PixelTweaksPublications.com

Printed by Ingram

Graphic Artwork by Sophie Bennett, Ulverston, Cumbria

How the Quiz Works

There are 30 sets of questions with answers on the following page.

There is no prescribed marking system.
Marks and prizes are at the discretion of the quizmaster.

Have Fun!

Contents

So, what do you know about Cumbria?

1. How many United Kingdom counties border Cumbria?

2. Which organisation is known by the acronym LDNPA?

3. When was William Wordsworth born? 1670, 1770 or 1870?

4. Which organisation designated the Lake District a World Heritage Site in 2017 – UNESCO, World Wildlife Fund or the European Landscape Convention?

5. What was the name of the 2015 storm which flooded 5,200 homes in Cumbria?

6. Cumbria has been awarded more Michelin Stars than any other county. True or False?

7. What proportion of the Lake District National Park is owned by the National Trust? One-fifth, one-half or two-thirds?

8. What was the population of Cumbria in 2019? 500,000, 750,000 or 950,000?

9. Which actress played the part of Beatrix Potter in the 2006 film Miss Potter?

10. When was the first confirmed case of COVID-19 reported in Cumbria? Was it February, March or April 2021?

Questions

So, what do you know about Cumbria?

1. **Six:** Lancashire; North Yorkshire; Durham, Northumberland; Scottish Borders; Dumfries and Galloway.

2. **Lake District National Park Authority**. Designated in May, confirmed August 1951, it is the largest National Park in England.

3. He was born in **Cockermouth in 1770** and died at Rydal Mount on 23rd April 1850. (Shakespeare's birthday!)

4. **UNESCO.** The Lake District is now a legally protected area "of outstanding value to humanity".

5. **Storm Desmond.** The cost of the damage in Cumbria was approximately £500 million.

6. **True.** In 2021 seven establishments in Cumbria were the holders of this award.

7. **One-fifth.** The National Trust owns 90 farms in the Lake District and about 70% of the world's Herdwick sheep.

8. **500,000.** The population is sparse, with 73.4 people per km².

9. **Renee Zellweger.** Ewan McGregor played Norman Warne, the publisher who died shortly before they were to be married.

10. **4th March.** UK lockdown measures came into force on 26th March 2020.

Answers

History, Ancient and Modern

1. Birkrigg, Swinside and Elva Plain are examples of which type of ancient monument?

2. When was Cumbria ruled by the kings of Rheged?

3. In which century did the Romans first occupy Carlisle and the borders of North West England?

4. Which invaders introduced the words 'fell' and 'beck' into our vocabulary?

5. Which commodity did the monks at St Bees begin mining in the 13th century?

6. What name was given to the lawless brigands who raided the borders between the 13th and 17th centuries?

7. "Is there no nook of English ground secure / From rash assault?" William Wordsworth wrote this in 1844. Why was he angry?

8. Which town was blitzed by the Luftwaffe in April and May, 1941?

9. The worst nuclear disaster in British history occurred in Cumbria in 1957. What happened and where?

10. In what year was Liberal Democrat, Tim Farron, elected MP for Westmorland and Lonsdale? 2000, 2005 or 2010?

Questions

History, Ancient and Modern

1. **Prehistoric stone circles.** There are approximately 50 in Cumbria.

2. **In the post-Roman era and early Middle Ages.** The history of Rheged has come down through a mixture of legend, genealogy and archeology.

3. **1st century AD.** Construction of Hadrian's Wall began the following century.

4. **The Vikings.** The words 'beck' and 'fell' are from the Old Norse 'bekkr' and 'fjallr'.

5. **Coal.** Seven lucrative centuries of mining on the west coast of Cumbria followed.

6. **The Border Reivers.** Mutual hatred between the English and Scots led to 300 years of violent looting and destruction.

7. He had learnt that **a railway line** from Kendal to Windermere was to be opened.

8. **Barrow-in-Furness.** 10,000 houses were damaged, which accounted for 25% of the housing stock.

9. A **fire broke out at Windscale** (now known as Sellafield). It ranked Level 5 out of 7 on the International Nuclear Event Scale.

10. **2005.** He fought three general elections, in Durham and Ribble South, before winning the seat.

Answers

Alfred Wainwright's 214

1. How many volumes are there in Wainwright's series *A Pictorial Guide to the Lakeland Fells*?

2. Which is the highest of Wainwright's 214 peaks and which is the lowest?

3. An Ambleside vet broke the record for completing Wainwright's 214 peaks in one circuit in June 2021. What is her name?

4. Which fell illustrates the cover of *Book Three, The Central Fells* – High Raise, Eagle Crag or Helm Crag?

5. In alphabetical order which Wainwright is the first and which the last?

6. In Scotland, how many Wainwrights would qualify as Munros? (Peaks listed by the Munro Society over 914m).

7. Which fell near Windermere was the first fell Wainwright climbed in the Lake District?

8. Which fell, according to Wainwright, offered the best reward for the effort required to climb it? Green Gable, Eel Crag or Hopegill Head?

9. Is Black Combe a Wainwright?

10. Which Wainwright is thought to involve the steepest climb in the Lake District?

Questions

Alfred Wainwright's 214

1. **Seven:** Southern; Central Eastern; Far Eastern; Western; Northern; North Western.

2. **Scafell Pike** is the highest (978m /3209ft). The lowest is Castle Crag (290m/951.5ft).

3. **Sabrina Verjee.** She finished the 325 mile (523km) route in 5 days, 23 hours and 49 minutes.

4. **Helm Crag.** It is 23rd out of 27 in order of altitude in the volume.

5. **Allen Crags** (Southern Fells) is the first and Yoke (Far Eastern Fells), the last.

6. **Four:** Scafell Pike; Scafell; Helvellyn; Skiddaw.

7. **Orrest Head** (237.7m/780ft), which he climbed in 1930 at the age of 23.

8. **Hopegill Head** the route from Coledale Hause via Hobcarton Crag.

9. **No.** It appears in *The Outlying Fells of Lakeland*. 'Wainwrights' are defined as those listed in the 7 Pictorial Guides. (Orrest Head is similar. See Q7 above.)

10. **Kirk Fell, from Wasdale Head,** where the gradient is 42% or 1 in 2.4 for a mile of the climb.

Answers

Yan Tan Tethera

1. Yan, Tyan, Tethera, - one, two, three, in the sheep counting rhyme. Which number does 'bumfit' denote?

2. What is meant when a Cumbrian describes something as 'L'al'?

3. You would be insulted if you were called a 'cuthbert'. What does it mean?

4. If a Cumbrian asked, "Hasta iver deeked a cuddy loup a five bar yat?" What would they want to know?

5. Who or what is your best 'marra'?

6. Which Tyne Tees and Border TV programme is known in dialect as 'Border Crack an Deekabout'?

7. There are a few dialect expressions for 'raining'. Which of the following does not mean raining —'Yukken', 'Liggin', 'Hossin' or 'Syling'?

8. By what name were the people of Westmorland once known?

9. 'Jack's Rake' is found in the Langdales, 'High Nun Rake' is in Dentdale. What does the word 'rake' signify?

10. If you won the lottery you would be 'spawney' in Cumbrian dialect. What does that mean?

Questions

Yan Tan Tethera

1. **Fifteen.** Bumfit is used in most Cumbrian dialects, apart from in High Furness where the word for fifteen is 'mimph'.

2. **Small.** It is often given to house names and can be written 'la'l', 'l'al' or la'al'!

3. **An idiot** – ouch!

4. "Have you ever seen a donkey jump a five bar gate?" Interesting question!

5. **Your best friend or mate.**

6. **Lookaround** - it has been broadcasting local news since the late 1960s.

7. **'Liggin'.** It means lying down. 'Liggin Kessin' describes a sheep which has fallen onto its back.

8. **Westmerians.** The county name was once spelt Westmereland.

9. **A steep lane or track**. Rakes were often part of the old droving roads.

10. **Lucky!**

Answers

Cumbrian Scribblers

1. *The Dove Cottage Journal* is the name of Dorothy Wordsworth's diary. True or False?

2. A poet relative of Samuel Taylor Coleridge lived at Greta Hall. What was his name?

3. After a tour of Cumberland, two famous Victorian novelists wrote *The Lazy Tour of Two Idle Apprentices*. Who were they?

4. Where, in Cumbria, was the home of journalist and social theorist Harriet Martineau?

5. An author, brought up in Cumbria, has written biographies of George Eliot, Sarah Losh and Edward Lear. What is her name?

6. What was the name of the Millom-born poet, 1914-1987?

7. This writer and Radio 6 DJ writes a column in *Cumbria Life* Magazine? What is his name?

8. Which Carlisle-born author (1938-2016) wrote *Georgy Girl* and *The Diary of an Ordinary Woman*?

9. Chris Pilling, Neil Curry and Kim Moore are writers in which genre?

10. Name the author of *The Coffin Trail* and *The Cipher Garden* in the Lake District Mystery series

Questions

Cumbrian Scribblers

1. **False.** The diary was called *The Grasmere Journal.* Some think her writing was as good as her brother's.

2. **Robert Southey.** His tomb in Crosthwaite Churchyard was restored by the Brazilian government in recognition of the history he wrote of Brazil.

3. **Charles Dickens and Wilkie Collins.** They came sightseeing in 1857.

4. **Ambleside.** Princess Victoria invited Harriet Martineau to her coronation in 1838.

5. **Jenny Uglow OBE.** She wrote *The Pine Cone,* the story of Sarah Losh who designed and rebuilt the church at Wreay, near Carlisle.

6. **Norman Nicholson OBE.** Easily distinguished by his fine mutton chop whiskers.

7. **Stuart Maconie.** Maconie's first love was fronting his band, Les Flirts.

8. **Margaret Forster.** She had a reclusive nature — rarely giving interviews.

9. **Poets.** All appeared in *THIS PLACE I KNOW, A New Anthology of Cumbrian Poetry.* Published in 2018 by Handstand Press.

10. **Martin Edwards.** To date (2021) he has published 8 books in the series.

Answers

Country Ways

1. Lovers Lonning, Fat Lonning and Squeezed Gut Lonning are all found in Cumbria, but what is a 'lonning'?

2. Which Victorian social pioneer encouraged the revival of country crafts in Cumbria?

3. Sheep in the Lake District are referred to as 'hefted'. What does that mean?

4. Which disease affecting cloven-hooved animals broke out in Cumbria in 2001?

5. *English Pastoral* is the second of James Rebanks' autobiographical accounts of hill farming in the Lakes. What was his first book called?

6. Which Cumbrian craft is associated with making wooden artefacts such as hurdles, rakes, bobbins and tool handles?

7. Which country show is held at Crooklands Showground every year?

8. Which region in Cumbria farms the most sheep? Is it Eden or South Lakeland?

9. John Graves wrote a song in the 1820's about his Cumbrian hunting friend. What was the song called?

10. An important part of a dry stone wall is the stoop. What is a stoop?

Questions

Country Ways

1. **A country lane.** Check out Alan Cleaver's book *The Lonnings of Cumbria* .

2. **John Ruskin.** He championed traditional skills of woodworking and linen craft as part of a rural arts revival.

3. **Hefted sheep** are rooted to a place on common land which they return to by instinct.

4. **Foot and mouth disease.** During the outbreak over a million sheep were slaughtered in Cumbria.

5. ***The Shepherd's Life.*** In 2021 *English Pastoral* won the Wainwright Prize for Nature Writing.

6. **Coppice craft.** Young trees are cut down each year, producing long straight shoots from which to fashion tools.

7. **The Westmorland County Show.** The show was established in 1799.

8. **Eden with over 700,000 sheep.** South Lakeland has 500,000. (Data from the June agricultural industry survey 2016)

9. **'D'ye ken John Peel.** John Peel was a famous huntsman. This song made him even more famous.

10. It is the **upright standing stone** at the wall head, where the wall ends or a gate is built.

Answers

Celebrities, past and present

1. Who was the legendary last king of Cumbria?

2. A Cockermouth-born sailor led a mutiny in 1789. Who was he and what was the name of the mutiny?

3. Hugh Lowther, 5th Lord Lonsdale had a nick-name. Was it the Red, Yellow or Blue Earl?

4. Which mountaineer completed the first solo ascent of Napes Needle, on Great Gable, in 1886?

5. True or False? Donald Campbell broke the world water speed record on Ullswater in 1955.

6. What title did Melvyn Bragg take on becoming a life peer in 2018? Baron Bragg of .....?

7. Name the Ulverston-born saxophonist who performed at the Last Night of the Proms in 2018.

8. Which fell runner organised the Kentmere Horseshoe Race for 40 years and ran a Kendal running equipment store?

9. This former Emmerdale actress and reality show celebrity was born in Carlisle in 1982. Can you name her?

10. Which journalist, brought up in Carlisle, wrote the first authorised biography of the Beatles?

Questions

Celebrities, past and present

1. **Dunmail.** A cinema and shopping centre in Workington is named after him.

2. **Fletcher Christian** — the Mutiny on the Bounty. Christian fled to Pitcairn Island in the Pacific where he probably died.

3. **The Yellow Earl.** With a passion for all things yellow, he dressed his servants in the colour and owned a yellow Rolls-Royce.

4. **Walter Parry Haskett Smith.** He is known as the father of British Rock Climbing.

5. **True.** He achieved a speed of 202.32 mph. He set four new records later on Coniston.

6. **Wigton,** where his childhood was spent.

7. **Jess Gillam.** Her first job was as a waitress at her parents' tea rooms in Ulverston.

8. **Pete Bland** (1941-2020). He founded his famous sports shop in 1971.

9. **Roxanne Pallett.** She played Jo Stiles in Emmerdale from 2005-2008.

10. **Hunter Davies.** He lived for many years in Loweswater with his wife, Margaret Forster.

Answers

Getting from A to B

1. In which decade was the Cumbria Way established?
   1960s, 1970s or 1980s?

2. Which Cumbrian pass connects Seatoller and
   Buttermere?

3. Which fell is named after the Roman road that crossed
   its summit?

4. How many kilometers of footpaths, bridleways, permitted
   paths and byways are there in the Lake District National
   Park? 1200km, 2,200km or 3,200km?

5. Do you know where the Westmorland Way starts and
   finishes?

6. What is the name of the bridge over the River Lune at
   Kirkby Lonsdale?

7. Which railway line crosses Cumbria and the Pennines en
   route for Leeds?

8. There are four places on Ullswater where you can catch
   an Ullswater Steamer. Can you name them?

9. The Lancaster Canal which opened in 1819, connected
   which Cumbrian town with industrial Lancashire?

10. What is the number of the west coast road running from
    Dalton-in-Furness to Carlisle?

Questions

Getting from A to B

1. **1970s.** It was devised by the Ramblers Association.

2. **Honister Pass.** It reaches an altitude of 356m/1.167 ft with a gradient of up to 1-in-4 (25%).

3. **High Street.** It was built in the 2nd century to link forts Voreda and Galava.

4. **3.200km** — 3,203km to be exact. Foot erosion is a problem. 'Fix the Fells' is a project to repair 344 upland paths.

5. **It starts in Ambleside and finishes in Arnside.** It is a low level route,145km long.

6. **Devil's Bridge.** Its name derives from a folk tale about an old lady who outwitted the devil.

7. **Settle to Carlisle.** It was opened to goods in 1875 and passengers in 1876.

8. **Glenridding, Howtown, Pooley Bridge and Aira Force Pier.** The ferry operates 363 days of the year.

9. **Kendal.** Sections are navigable but other parts were severed during the construction of the M6.

10. **A595.** At Dalton it joins the A590. In central Carlisle it becomes Castle Way.

Answers

Food and Drink

1. The largest Cumberland sausage was made in Broughton-in-Furness in 2012. Did it weigh 130kg, 135kg, or 140kg?

2. Stiff drinks are on offer at The Lakes Distillery. Where is it located?

3. Which is the oldest Kendal Mint Cake maker — Quiggin's, Romney's or Wilson's?

4. On which TV programme has Cumbrian food critic Grace Dent regularly appeared — Masterchef, The Great British Bake Off or Hell's Kitchen?

5. In 1854 Sarah Nelson of Grasmere created a unique recipe. What was it for?

6. Which publication runs the annual Cumbria Food and Drinks Awards?

7. There are tasty things to relish in Hawkshead. What are they?

8. What will you find at Plumgarths, near Kendal? An orchard, a farm shop or plum pie makers?

9. Which village, associated with shrimp and cockle fishing, is home to the Lakeland Willow Water company?

10. In which South Lakeland town is Farrer's, said to be the oldest coffee roaster in the UK?

Questions

Food and Drink

1. **135kg.** Surprise surprise - it was a Guinness World Record winner!

2. **Close to the shores of Bassenthwaite.** It produces Cumbrian whisky, gin and vodka.

3. **Quiggin's**. This company was established in 1840. Wilson's is owned by the Windermere firm McClures

4. **Masterchef.** Her memoir *Hungry*, was published in 2020.

5. **Gingerbread.** Her grave is close to Wordsworth's tomb in St. Oswald's Churchyard, Grasmere.

6. *Cumbria Life Magazine.* Awards are made in 14 categories, from Specialist Retailer to Best Newcomer.

7. **Hawkshead Relish** Company's award-winning chutneys and preserves.

8. **A farm shop**, specialising in locally-sourced produce. There's a café there too.

9. **Flookburgh.** The village's name is thought to derive from the Norse name Flugga – ie Flugga's town.

10. **Kendal**. Farrer's opened a tea and coffee warehouse there in1819.

Answers

Creative Endeavour

1. Terry Abraham's TV film series, *Life of a Mountain*, features three Lakeland peaks. Which ones?

2. Colin Telfer's sculpted figure of a lamplighter stands on a West Cumbrian street. Which one?

3. Beatrix Potter's 'Peter Rabbit' has been made into a TV series and a film - true or false?

4. The Lake District was the location of a spectacular scene in which *Star Wars* film?

5. What nationality was the artist Kurt Schwitters who settled in Ambleside in 1945?

6. Where, in Cumbria, is handmade lead crystal glassware made?

7. This artist, married to Ben Nicholson, spent 70 years painting in Cumbria. Who was she?

8. In which year was Printfest in Ulverston founded? 2001, 2008 or 2011?

9. Which museum in Ambleside houses a collection of Beatrix Potter's illustrations?

10. A venue near Penrith houses a puppet theatre, art gallery and café. What is its name?

Questions

Creative Endeavour

1. **Scafell Pike** (2014), **Blencathra** (2016) and **Helvellyn** (2021).

2. **Senhouse Street, Maryport.** Telfer worked in Cumbrian collieries as a winding engineer. His sculptures depict working people.

3. **True.** Peter Rabbit, the 56 episode TV series began in 2012. Peter Rabbit, the film was released in 2018.

4. ***Star Wars: The Force Awakens.*** Cat Bells is the backdrop for one of its famous scenes.

5. **German.** Schwitters fled Germany in 1937 following the inclusion of his work in the Degenerate Art exhibition organised by the Nazis.

6. **Ulverston.** Cumbria Crystal was founded in 1976. It supplied crystal for the set of the TV series Downton Abbey.

7. **Winifred Nicholson** (1993-1981). She lived at Bankshead, near Hadrian's Wall.

8. **2011.** Founded by Judy Evans, and Ronkey Bullard, it attracts printmakers from all over the world.

9. **The Armitt.** Beatrix Potter studied and painted wildlife, particularly fungi.

10. **Upfront.** John and Elaine Parkinson opened the venue in 1997 in a property known as Unthank Hall.

Answers

Water, Water, Everywhere

1. What is the average volume of water in Windermere? 300bn litres, 30bn litres or 3bn litres?

2. Scale Force, near Crummock Water, has the highest waterfall drop in the Lake District. True or False?

3. What is the speed limit on the lakes which permit the use of powered watercraft?

4. Is Devoke Water a lake or a tarn according to the Lake District National Park Authority?

5. What did Lord Birkett do to 'save' Ullswater in 1962?

6. Which lake's name comes from the old norse 'laufsær'— meaning 'leaves' ?

7. Derwentwater's deepest point is deeper than Windermere's, true or false?

8. Which tarn, in a hollow between Tarn Crag and Blea Rigg, flows into Sourmilk Gill?

9. There are at least six tarns/waters in Cumbria with the name 'Blea' in them. What do you think it means?

10. Caldbeck is named after the river on which is stands — Cald Beck. True or False?

Questions

Water, Water, Everywhere

1. **300bn litres.** Windermere is 10.5 miles long and the largest lake in the Lake District.

2. **True.** It has a single drop of 170ft followed by two 20ft drops.

3. **10mph.** Five lakes permit powered watercraft — Derwent Water, Windermere, Coniston Water, Ullswater and Bassenthwiate.

4. **Devoke Water is a tarn.** We take LDNPA's word for it!

5. **He campaigned** to overturn a proposal to turn Ullswater into a reservoir.

6. **Loweswater.** Owned by the National Trust and, only a mile long, it is one of the smallest lakes.

7. **False.** Derwentwater is one of the shallowest lakes. Its deepest point is 22m.

8. **Easedale Tarn.** It has always been a popular spot. The Victorians built a refreshment hut there.

9. 'Blea' comes from the Old Norse, meaning **dark blue**.

10. **True.** More of a river than a beck, it powered many local mills in the 17th and 18th centuries.

Answers

Border Country

1. Which part of the Irish Sea separates the coast of Cumbria from the coast of Dumfries and Galloway?

2. Why is the 1237 treaty of York significant in border history?

3. What name is given to the towers built as a defense against border raiders between the 13th and 17th centuries?

4. Which former MP for Penrith and The Border published an account in 2017 of a journey with his father through the borderlands?

5. What is the name of the border river on which Gretna stands?

6. True or false — Hadrian's Wall marked the northernmost frontier of the Roman Empire?

7. What road does the M6 become after J45?

8. What is the name of the part of Kielder Forest which lies in Cumbria and borders Scotland?

9. What name was given to the independent disputed borderland between England and Scotland from the 12th century?

10. The 'Welcome to Scotland' motorway sign is also written in gaelic. How does it translate?

Questions

Border Country

1. **The Solway Firth.** Between 1868 and 1921 it was crossed by a 1780m long railway viaduct.

2. Signed by Henry III and Alexander II, it **defined most of what remains the Anglo-Scottish border** today.

3. **Peel or Pele Towers.** Many survive as part of old houses and castles, such as Penrith Castle.

4. **Rory Stewart.** The book was titled *The Marches: Border Walks with My Father.*

5. **The River Sark.** The English were defeated by the Scots at the Battle of Sark in 1448.

6. **False.** The Roman Antonine Wall marks the northernmost frontier, approximately 150km north of Hadrian's Wall.

7. **The A74(M).** The motorway system continues north from here, ending at Perth.

8. **Kershope forest.** It is part of Cumbria's most northern uplands.

9. **The Debatable Lands.** Scots' Dike, built in 1552, settled the boundary between them .

10. **'Fàilte Gu Alba'.** (An extra point for spelling it correctly!)

Answers

By the Seaside

1. The Solway coast is a designated AONB. What is an AONB?

2. This headland marks Cumbria's westernmost point. Can you name it?

3. Which two river estuaries define the Furness Peninsula?

4. Ravenglass is the only coastal town in the Lake District National Park. True or False?

5. From which coastal town does the River Derwent flow into the Irish Sea - Workington or Whitehaven?

6. A Seascale landmark is a Grade II listed Victorian Tower. Why was it built – as an aid to navigation, a water tower or a war memorial?

7. The King of Piel Island, usually the pub landlord, offers his appointed knights free lodging in return for what?

8. What is the shortest approximate distance from the coast of Cumbria to the Isle of Man?

9. This former industrial village near Barrow has an old pier built from iron slag, jutting out into the Duddon estuary. Name the village.

10. There's something 'boring' about Arnside. What is it?

Questions

By the Seaside

1. **Area of Outstanding Natural Beauty.** It was designated in 1964.

2. **St Bees Head.** St Bega is said to have landed here from Ireland in AD850.

3. **The Leven and the Duddon.** The River Leven merges with the Crake at Greenodd before joining the estuary.

4. **True.** The natural harbour at Ravenglass was an important Roman naval base.

5. **Workington.** It rises at Sprinkling Tarn and flows through Derwentwater and Bassenthwaite.

6. **A water tower.** It was built by the Furness Railway in 1878 to supply water to a proposed housing estate nearby.

7. **A round of drinks for every customer in the bar.** It guarantees knights a bed in the pub should they become shipwrecked.

8. **Just under 50km** — the distance between St Bees Head and the Point of Ayre on the Isle of Man.

9. **Askam-in-Furness.** It is the home of the Duddon Inshore Rescue.

10. **The Arnside Bore.** A fast moving tidal bore passes close to the village on spring tides.

Answers

Words, words, words!

1. Complete Norman Nicholson's book title: *The Lakers. The Adventures of the First ...*

2. In October 1802, which diarist wrote "rose fresh and well - at a little after 8 o'clock I saw them go down the avenue towards the Church."?

3. "Oh God ,... I know not how to proceed, how to return." Name the poet who wrote this after getting stuck on Scafell in 1802.

4. Who dedicated one of his guide books to 'The Sheep of Lakeland'?

5. Where will you find this inscription? "The first aeroplane to land on a mountain in Great Britain did so on this spot on December 22nd 1926."

6. "We were working class ... Later on I bolted on media middle class ... and now people like me are in the House of Lords." Who wrote this?

7. Who wrote, "I'm sorry to say that Peter was not very well during the evening."?

8. "BETTER DROWNED THAN DUFFERS IF NOT DUFFERS WON'T DROWN." Name the author and the novel.

9. "The moment I catch sight of the Monument I say to myself, "At last I am home again". Which judge wrote this on returning to Ulverston?

10. Complete this book title by Karen Lloyd. *The Gathering Tide. A Journey around the Edgelands of ...*

Questions

Words, words, words!

1. *.....Tourists*. Published in 1955, it ends hoping that humans learn to live in harmony with the natural world.

2. **Dorothy Wordsworth** on her brother William's wedding day. Overcome with emotion she went back to bed!

3. **Samuel Taylor Coleridge.** He took the wrong route from the summit onto the notorious rock formation, Broad Stand.

4. **Alfred Wainwright.** In Book Four, *The Southern Fells,* he wrote, 'Dedicated to the hardiest of all fellwalkers, The Sheep of Lakeland'.

5. **On the summit of Helvellyn.** Pilots Bert Hinkler and John Leeming landed there on their third attempt.

6. **Lord Melvyn Bragg.** His father was a pub landlord in Wigton.

7. **Beatrix Potter** - of course! *The Tale of Peter Rabbit*, published in 1902, was the first of 23 books in the series.

8. **Arthur Ransome** in *Swallows and Amazons*. These words from their father, are sent in a telegram to the children to encourage them in their exploits.

9. **Norman Birkett, KC.** He was a high court judge and Second British Judge at the Nuremburg Trials.

10. *... Morecambe Bay.*' Karen Lloyd is a native of Cumbria and a passionate conservationist.

Answers

On the Wild Side

1. Which Cumbrian area reports most red squirrel sightings according to RSNE (Red Squirrels Northern England)?

2. Cumbria is home to a species of bird renowned for the speed of its hunting dive – the fastest in the world. Which bird?

3. This mammal breeds on the shores of Walney Island. Can you name it?

4. Otters are extinct in Cumbria. True or False?

5. Willow trees are being planted in Cumbria to help slow erosion. Is willow native to Cumbria?

6. Where on the Furness Peninsula do ospreys return in March each year to nest?

7. Which wetland flower is the county flower of Cumbria? It's the one on the Cumberland flag. (We're impressed if you know this!)

8. Which area in Cumbria has the least light pollution in the county?

9. Pike? Perch? Trout? Which is the largest freshwater fish you can catch in Cumbria?

10. Large areas of salt marsh lie in the north and south of the county. Whereabouts?

Questions

On the Wild Side

1. **Penrith and North-East Lakeland.** It's helpful to report sightings to a red squirrel protection group (see RSNE website).

2. **The peregrine falcon.** It dives at speeds of up to 200mph.

3. **The grey seal.** It is the only place they breed in Cumbria.

4. **False.** Having come close to extinction they are rare but increasingly widespread.

5. **Yes.** Planted closely, willows form a tight net of roots which hold the soil together.

6. **Foulshaw Moss.** Visit cumbriawildlifetrust.org.uk/wildlife/cams/osprey-cam to watch their activity online.

7. **The grass of parnassus, or 'bog star'.** It is also the county flower of Sutherland in Scotland.

8. **The tripoint between Scotland, Cumbria, and Northumberland.** It has only 19.9 micro candelas of artificial light per square metre.

9. **Pike.** A pike was caught at Esthwaite Water weighing 46lbs.

10. **The Solway Coast and Grange-Over-Sands.** Salt marsh is a wetland formed from an accumulation of sand and silt from the tides.

Answers

Mysterious Cumbria

1. What is the legend of Long Meg and her Daughters?

2. Many myths link King Arthur with Cumbria. Which city in Cumbria is thought to be Camelot's location?

3. The dialect poem, *The Fell King*, reimagines the fells as people. Which fell is cast as King?

4. Why might it be scary walking the western shores of Windermere after dark?

5. How many reports of ghosts, aliens and big cat sightings were received by the police between 2017 and 2020?

6. Mary Baines, the Tebay Witch, predicted the arrival, 30 years after her death, of 'horseless carriages'. Was she correct?

7. In which valley, according to legend, were the Normans defeated in the 12th century by Britons and Norsemen.

8. Name Muncaster Castle's famous ghostie? Is it Tom Fool, Sad Tom or Tom Teaser?

9. "My crown – bear it away, never let the Saxon flout it, until I come to lead you". Who said this?

10. Does the dialect word 'dobbie' mean a haunted house, a ghost, or a wishing well?

Questions

Mysterious Cumbria

1. **They were turned into a stone circle** for practicing pagan rituals on the Sabbath.

2. **Carlisle.** Arthuret Church near Longtown claims to be Arthur's burial place.

3. **Scafell.** The 1876 poem tells of an argument between Helvellyn and Skiddaw over who should be the king. They finally agree on Scafell.

4. **The Crier of Claife**, a lovelorn Monk, haunts the wooded hillside crying out for his lost love.

5. **500.** The majority were of big cats (448 calls).

6. **The railway came to Tebay** in 1846, 35 years after she died. Spooky!

7. **Rannerdale.** Nicholas Size made the story famous in his 1930 novel *The Secret Valley.*

8. **Tom Fool.** Other ghosts at the castle include Mary Bragg who was murdered there in the 19th century.

9. **Dunmail, King of Cumbria.** His words were in vain as Cumbria eventually became part of England.

10. **A ghost.** A dobbie is said to haunt the roads near Bardsea on the Furness Peninsula.

Answers

The Ground Beneath Our Feet

1. How many years ago was Cumbria glaciated? 1,100 years, 11,000 years or 110,000 years?

2. Which group of rocks in northern Cumbria was formed from the mud and sand which settled on the seabed 500 million years ago?

3. Is Cumbria's groundwater harder or softer than the average in England?

4. Many rocks in Cumbria are siltstone. Is siltstone a sedimentary, igneous or metamorphic rock?

5. The largest cavern in Cumbria lies in the quarries of Little Langdale. What is its name?

6. Are the Lake District fells older or younger than the Himalayas?

7. What metamorphic rock, popular for roofing, is mined at Honister?

8. Where, in Cumbria, was the epicentre of the earthquake of 28th April 2009?

9. Striding Edge is an example of an 'arête'. What is an 'arête'?

10. Which ore of iron has been extensively mined from the limestone layers of western Cumbria?

Questions

The Ground Beneath Our Feet

1. **11,000 years ago.** Before the ice melted at the end of the last Ice Age Morecambe Bay was dry land,

2. **The Skiddaw Group.** They are the oldest rocks in the Lake District.

3. **Softer.** Reduced limescale in the groundwater is due to a lack of limestone in the bedrock.

4. **Sedimentary.** It formed on or near the Earth's surface.

5. **Cathedral Cave.** It is 40ft high – one of a series of interlinked caves and tunnels. Take a torch!

6. **They are older.** The Himalayas were formed on a collisional plate boundary 50 million years ago. The Borrowdale Volcanic Group formed 450 million years ago!

7. **Slate.** Slate forms from shale after many years of intense heat and pressure.

8. **Close to Ulverston.** It measured 3.7 on the Richter Scale equating to II or III on the Mercalli Scale.

9. **A glacial ridge,** specifically one separating two valleys. 'Arête' is the French word for 'edge' or 'ridge'.

10. **Haematite.** There is evidence of iron ore mining in West Cumbria as early as 1179.

Answers

Landmarks

In which centuries were these Cumbrian landmarks built?

1. The Gosforth Cross
2. The Countess Pillar
3. Ravenglass Bath House
4. Smardale Gill Viaduct.
5. Furness Abbey
6. Edward I Monument
7. Pendragon Castle
8. The Whitehaven Lighthouses
9. Sellafield.
10. Hamspfell Hospice

Questions

Landmarks

1. **A 10th century** Anglo-Saxon cross in St. Mary's Churchyard, Gosforth.

2. **17th century**. It is at Brougham castle where Lady Anne Clifford parted from her mother in 1616.

3. **The 2nd century** Roman bath house is one of the tallest surviving Roman buildings in the UK.

4. **19th century.** The railway viaduct near Kirkby Stephen, built in1861, carried coke to furnaces in Barrow and West Cumberland.

5. The Abbey was founded in the **12th century** by Stephen, Count of Boulogne, later King of England.

6. The **17th century** monument was built on the Solway coast in 1685 to commemorate Edward Longshanks who died there in 1307.

7. Built by the Normans in the **12th century** near Kirkby Stephen. Some believe it was founded by Uther Pendragon, King Arthur's father.

8. Whitehaven's lighthouses were built in the **19th century**; one on the west pier in 1839 and one on the north pier in 1941.

9. A **20th century** government site, now used for reprocessing nuclear fuel, nuclear waste storage and nuclear decommissioning.

10. A **19th century** folly on Hampsfell built to shelter travellers.

Answers

A Grand Day Out

1. This visitor attraction celebrates everything Cumbrian. Is it Finerid, Hagrid or Rheged?

2. Which Roman fort sits on the longest remaining stretch of Hadrian's Wall in Cumbria?

3. This favourite fell may have got its name from 'cat's bield'. The word 'bield' is Old English for shelter. Which fell is it?

4. A Cumbrian castle is the backdrop for the Kendal Calling music festival. Which castle?

5. A Jacobean mansion in Carlisle houses a museum and art gallery. What is its name?

6. Which town is home to the Dock Museum? Whitehaven, Silloth or Barrow-in-Furness?

7. Which annual summer art exhibition traditionally draws over 10,000 visitors?

8. How many tourists does the LDNPA estimate visit the Lake District every year?

9. Roman altars and sculptures are on display at this museum in Maryport. What is its name?

10. Where, on the shores of Windermere, can you climb through the trees and try archery and laser clay shooting?

Questions

A Grand Day Out

1. **Rheged.** It was built by the Westmorland Group who own Tebay services.

2. **Birdoswald.** It was founded cira112AD and abandoned circa 500 AD.

3. **Cat Bells.** It is a 451 metre climb on the western shores of Derwentwater.

4. **Lowther Castle.** The family, unable to meet death duties, demolished much of the building after WW2.

5. **Tullie House.** The gallery owns an important collection of Pre-Raphaelite art.

6. **Barrow-in-Furness.** The museum opened on its new site in the old dockyard in 1994.

7. **The Lake Artist's Society.** The society held its first exhibition in 1904.

8. **Almost 15.8 million.** The pandemic of 2020/21 cost The Lake District's economy £1.5 billion, cutting the tourism industry in half, with the loss of 20,000 jobs.

9. **Senhouse Roman Museum.** Many objects were discovered during an excavation nearby.

10. **Brockhole, The Lake District Visitor Centre.** There's enough to do there to keep you busy all day.

Answers

Off the Beaten Track

1. Is Seathwaite on Morecambe Bay, in the Duddon Valley, or close to Whitehaven?

2. Is Hesket Newmarket north-west, south-west or due east of Penrith?

3. On which railway line does Foxfield lie — Settle to Carlisle, Eden Valley or the Cumbrian Coast Line?

4. Where in Furness is Vickerstown — on Roa Island, Barrow Island or Walney Island?

5. Mardale Green was flooded to create a reservoir. Was it Thirlmere, Haweswater or Wet Sleddale?

6. On which Lakeland shore does Rannerdale lie? Is it Crummock Water, Ennerdale Water or Buttermere?

7. What makes Bewcastle an historic site? Is it the Bewcastle Cross, the Bewcastle Stone Circle or Bewcastle Castle?

8. What is manufactured in Burneside near Kendal? Is it pickles, paper or pumps?

9. Where is Newton Arlosh? Is it near Silloth, near Seascale or near St. Bees?

10. The Mighty Mortal, The Mere Mortal, The Mortal Man? Which of these is the name of a pub in Troutbeck?

Questions

Off the Beaten Track

1. **The Duddon Valley.** Robert Walker, the 'Wonderful Walker', 1709-1802, was vicar there for 66 years.

2. **North-west.** Hesket Newmarket Brewery Cooperative brews a popular range of real ale there.

3. **Cumbrian Coast Line.** When it opened in 1848 the station was called Foxfield Junction.

4. **Walney Island.** It was built in the early 20th century for workers from Vickers shipyard (now BAE systems).

5. **Haweswater.** Mardale Green was flooded in 1935.

6. **Crummock Water.** In May thousands of visitors come to see the bluebells at Rannerdale Knott.

7. **Bewcastle Cross and Bewcastle Castle.** The cross is Anglo-Saxon. The Medievel castle stands on the site of a Roman Fort.

8. **Paper.** James Cropper plc has made paper in Burneside since 1845.

9. **Near Silloth.** Newton Arlosh is on the B5307. It was on the old drovers' road to Carlisle. (Read *The Drover's Boy*, by Irvine Hunt).

10. **The Mortal Man.** The pub was a favourite watering hole of Wordsworth and his contemporaries.

Answers

Fun and Games

1. Which South Cumbrian football team was promoted to the Football League in 2020?

2. 'Up and Unders', 'Uppies and Downies', 'Uppers and Overs'. Which of these is played in Workington?

3. In which Cumbrian town was the Snowsports Club founded in 1984?

4. In which sport does Cumbrian Georgia Stanway represent England?

5. A via ferrata has been installed on Honister Crag. What is a 'via ferrata'?

6. Which Cumbrian ski club is proud to have the longest ski lift in England?

7. Rugby players, James Botham, Phil Dowson and John Spencer went to the same school in Cumbria. Which one?

8. Which top Cumbrian climber is also a para-alpinist?

9. In which sport is the Lord Birkett Memorial Cup competed for each year – cricket, sailing or rugby?

10. Whose home ground is Edenside, Carlisle – Cumbria County Cricket Club or Carlisle Football Club?

Questions

Fun and Games

1. **Barrow AFC.** They last played in the League in 1972.

2. **Uppies and Downies.** It is a mob form of football with very few rules.

3. **Kendal.** Two hundred locals donated £10 each to start the club.

4. **Football.** She began playing for England in 2018. She has also played for Man City.

5. **From the Italian for 'iron way'** it is a fixed iron climbing route on the crag face. Only for the brave!

6. **Yad Moss Ski Club.** The club operates a 600m tow on Yad Moss, in the North Pennines,

7. **Sedbergh School.** Botham, son of Ian, plays for Wales. Phil Dowson played for England in 2012. John Spencer played for England 1969-71.

8. **Leo Holding.** Also known as base jumping, this sport involves a climb and a parachute jump from the mountain summit.

9. **Sailing.** The annual race is held on Ullswater.

10. **Cumbria County Cricket Club.** They were Minor Counties Champions in 1986, 1999 and 2015.

Answers

Carlisle

1. A statue on Caldewgate is a tribute to the 'Cracker Packers' of Carlisle. Who were they?

2. Which king, son of William the Conqueror, elevated Carlisle Priory to the status of cathedral in 1133?

3. Where, on the outskirts of Carlisle, was the WWII RAF Airfield and Pilot Training School?

4. In 2001 Carlisle Council installed an inscribed granite slab in an underpass near the Cathedral. What is written there?

5. What is Carlisle railway station's official name?

6. Why did US President Woodrow Wilson make a 'pilgrimage of the heart' to Carlisle in 1918?

7. In which year was Carlisle city centre pedestrianised? 1979, 1989, 1999?

8. What was the Roman name for Carlisle?

9. What is the name of the old mill at Denton Holme, once the largest cotton mill in England?

10. A Radio Cumbria breakfast presenter who later worked on Blue Peter was born in Carlisle. Do you know her name?

Questions

Carlisle

1. **The women employed at Carr's Biscuit Factory** from 1831. Carrs is now part of United Biscuits.

2. **Henry I.** He wanted to show who was the boss of England's unruly northern borderland.

3. **Kingstown.** Tiger Moths and Miles Magisters were flown from RAF Kingstown, now an industrial estate known as Kingsmoor Park.

4. **A 16th century curse** invoked by Archbishop Dunbar against the Border Reivers.

5. **Carlisle Citadel, opened in 1847.** It played an important part in northern Britain's logistical efforts in WW1.

6. His mother, **Jesse Janet Woodrow, was born there** in 1826.

7. **1989.** The old city streets were redeveloped and opened as 'The Lanes' earlier in 1984.

8. **Luguvalium,** thought to mean 'stronghold of Lugus'. The name eventually became Carlisle from the Brythonic word 'Ker' meaning fort.

9. **Shaddon Mill.** Dixon's Chimney, the mill chimney named after its builder, was restored in 1999 and stands at 290ft.

10. **Helen Skelton.** Helen is also a qualified tap dance teacher!

Answers

Keswick

1. Which day is market day in Keswick?

2. What is the name of Keswick's weekly newspaper?

3. Which park in Keswick is home to Keswick Cricket Club and Keswick Museum and Art Gallery?

4. In which year did the railway line to Keswick close?

5. When is the Keswick Film Festival held?

6. What is the name of the small village on the western outskirts of Keswick where prehistoric remains were found in 1901?

7. Only one of the islands in Derwentwater is inhabited. Which one?

8. Which vicar, with his wife, founded the Keswick School of Industrial Arts?

9. What is the name of the cinema in St. John's Street in Keswick?

10. Which country has the most towns named Keswick?

Questions

Keswick

1. There are two, **Thursday and Saturday.**

2. *Keswick Reminder.* It has been published every Friday since 1896.

3. **Fitz Park.** In the museum, among other curiosities, there's Napoleon's tea cup and John Peel's rocking chair.

4. **The line closed in 1972** and is now part of the Coast to Coast Cycle Route.

5. **The end of February.** It hosts the Osprey Short Film Awards to recognise short films by local directors.

6. **Portinscale.** The name, from the Old English 'portcwene' and Old Norse for hut, translates to 'the harlot's hut'.

7. **Derwent Island.** The 18th century house was built by Joseph Pocklington. Wordsworth said it spoilt the view.

8. **Canon Rawnsley,** who began by offering woodwork and metalwork classes in the parish room at Crosthwaite.

9. **The Alhambra.** Established in 1913, it is one of Britain's earliest surviving cinemas.

10. **USA.** There are 6 places in the USA called Keswick. There are two other Keswicks in England - both in Norfolk.

Answers

Coniston

1. Which historic county did Coniston belong to before the 1974 boundary change?

2. Do you know how The Old Man of Coniston got its name?

3. Where, in Coniston, is the artist, naturalist and philosopher John Ruskin buried?

4. What is the name of the annual motor rally based in Coniston, Grizedale Forest and Broughton Moor?

5. What is the average rainfall in Coniston each year? 64mm, 604mm or 1604mm?

6. Until the 18th century Coniston Water was known by an alternative name. Do you know what it was?

7. Which event in 1859 helped Coniston become a popular tourist destination?

8. For which activity were the Coniston Tigers known? Cycling, Fell Running or Rock Climbing?

9. Which 400 year old coaching inn is home to the Coniston Brewing Company?

10. Who has fallen out over the restoration of Donald Campbell's speedboat Bluebird?

Questions

Coniston

1. **Lancashire.** Coniston was part of 'Lancashire North of the Sands'.

2. The words 'old man' are a corruption of the Celtic words **'alt maen'** meaning 'high stone'.

3. **St. Andrew's Churchyard.** He was offered burial at Westminster Abbey, but Coniston was his preferred resting place.

4. **The Grizedale Stages Rally.** 44 miles of racing take place in winter each year.

5. **1604mm.** The average temperature is 8.1°C. Brrrr!

6. **Thurston Water.** It was named after 'Thursteinn', an Old Norse personal name.

7. **The opening of a railway line.** The Furness Railway guide promised to "land the wayfarer in the romantic valley of Coniston".

8. **Rock climbing.** Harry Griffin and friends formed a climbing club in the 1930s.

9. **The Black Bull.** Pints brewed from Cumbrian water are served, such as Bluebird Bitter and Old Man Ale.

10. **Gina Campbell, his daughter, and the restorer, Bill Smith,** have argued over its ownership.

Answers

Kendal

1. Which arts venue in Kendal was rebranded in 2021?

2. Which newspaper is published in Kendal?

3. In which decade did the Kendal bypass and one-way system open through the town?

4. Where does the train line end on the service north-west through Kendal from Oxenholme?

5. In which month does the annual Lakes International Comic Art Fest normally take place in Kendal?

6. Which craft is on display at a Quaker Museum in Kendal?

7. At which battle against the French in 1415 did the archers of Kendal help to secure an English victory?

8. How many road bridges are there over the River Kent in Kendal?

9. Kendal is the site of two castles. What are their names?

10. Which lake is closest to Kendal?

Questions

Kendal

1. **Brewery Arts.** It was launched with a new logo, upgraded website and revamped restaurant.

2. *The Westmorland Gazette.* It celebrated its 200th anniversary in 2018.

3. **1970s.** The one-way system was introduced after the bypass opened. Before then the A6 ran through the centre of Kendal.

4. **Windermere.** The service was opened in 1846. It is a single track railway line.

5. **October.** The festival appoints a UK Comics Laureate to champion the work of comic artists.

6. **Tapestry.** The museum is housed in the original Georgian Quaker Meeting House.

7. **The Battle of Agincourt.** Archers wore 'Kendal Green' a tough woollen cloth woven in the town.

8. **Five:** Victoria Bridge, Miller Bridge, Stramongate Bridge, Romney Road Bridge and Nether Bridge.

9. **Kendal Castle and Castle Howe.** Castle Howe was a motte and bailey castle. Only the earthworks are visible.

10. **Windermere** - 8.8 miles from Kendal. Next closest are Coniston Water, 22.2 miles away and Haweswater, 24.2 miles.

Answers

Ulverston

1. Ulverston is twinned with two towns, Albert in France and Harlem, Georgia, USA. Why was the latter twinned with Ulverston?

2. What is the height of Hoad Hill?

3. Where in Ulverston was the Union Workhouse situated?

4. Hound trail, pigeon shooting and wrestling competitions were held at which event in Ulverston from 1835?

5. This family, who opened a grocery in Market Street in 1892, is still in business. What is their name?

6. What is the proper name of the Buddhist Centre at Conishead Priory?

7. Which arts company had its headquarters at Lantern House in Ulverston?

8. In which decade did work begin on creating the County Road, bypassing Ulverston town centre?

9. Which test match cricketer, born in Ulverston, made his test debut in 1964?

10. When did Glaxo SmithKline begin manufacturing pharmaceuticals in Ulverston. 1948, 1968 or 1988?

Questions

Ulverston

1. **Harlem was the birthplace of Oliver Hardy**, screen pal of Ulverston's Stan Laurel. A fine bit of history they've gotten themselves into.

2. **436ft/133m above sea level.** The monument is 100ft or 30.5 m high.

3. **Stanley Street.** It was built in 1837-8. By 1841 there were 168 inmates, 75 of whom were children under 16.

4. **Flan Sports.** Competitive pole vaulting is said to have been invented there.

5. **Gillam.** Doug and Shirley continue the tradition at their tea-room and specialist grocers.

6. **The Manjushri Kadampa Meditation Centre.** The Buddha Manjushri is the manifestation of all Buddhist wisdom.

7. **Welfare State International.** It was founded by John Fox and Sue Gill.

8. **1960s.** Many historic buildings were demolished during this period, including most of the old Market Hall and part of the Theatre Royal building.

9. **Norman Gifford.** He was a slow left-arm bowler

10. **1948.** The company announced the plant will close in 2025.

Answers

Appleby & Kirkby Stephen

1. Name the row of cairns close to the summit of Hartley Fell, near Kirkby Stephen.

2. A trail on the outskirts of Kirkby Stephen features verse inscribed on stones along the way. What is its name?

3. There's a stone footbridge over the Eden in Kirkby Stephen. Is it - Tom's Bridge. Lady Anne's Bridge, or Frank's Bridge?

4. Volunteers are restoring track on the old Eden Valley Railway. What is the group's name?

5. The parish church in Kirkby Stephen, known as the Cathedral of the Dales, is dedicated to which saint?

6. Caesar's Tower forms a part of an historic building in Appleby. Can you name it?

7. For what purpose was St. Anne's Hospital in Appleby founded in 1651?

8. In which month is the annual Appleby Horse Fair traditionally held?

9. The name Appleby derives from the Norse for 'town/farm with apple trees'. True or False?

10. Two half brothers of a future US President were sent to Appleby Grammar School in 1729. Which President?

Questions

Appleby & Kirkby Stephen

1. **Nine Standards Rigg.** They follow the line of the Coast to Coast Walk.

2. **The Poetry Path.** Carver, Pip Hall, has inscribed 12 stones with verse by Meg Peacocke. They describe a year in the life of a fellside farmer.

3. **Frank's Bridge.** A stone at each end allowed a resting place for coffins as they were carried to church.

4. **The Stainmore Railway Company Ltd.** It is restoring Kirkby Stephen East railway station.

5. It appears to have no official dedication although it is popularly known as **St. Stephen's.**

6. **Appleby Castle.** The 12th century tower was the original castle keep. The castle is privately owned.

7. **Alms Houses.** Lady Anne Clifford built them to house homeless women.

8. **It is held in June** and claims to be the largest Gypsy Fair in Europe.

9. **True.** The Vikings settled in the Eden Valley in the 9th century.

10. **George Washington.** George was due to attend but his father died and the family could not afford to send him.

Answers

Wigton, Whitehaven and Workington

1. An elaborate granite memorial stands in the market place in Wigton. Is it a statue, a fountain or an obelisk?

2. Broadcaster Anna Ford's father, Rev John Ford, was the rector of which Wigton church in the 1950s?

3. What is the name of the little theatre in Wigton run by volunteers?

4. The grandmother of a United States president lived in Whitehaven. Who was that President? Abraham Lincoln, George Washington or Thomas Jefferson?

5. The layout of Whitehaven is predominantly Georgian. True or False?

6. What is the name of the museum situated on Whitehaven Harbour?

7. Workington is the start of a Sea to Sea Cycle Route. Where does the route finish?

8. What is meant by the term 'Workington Man'?

9. This Queen, in disguise, sought refuge in Workington in 1568. Who was she?

10. What is the name of the footbridge in Workington destroyed in the 2009 floods and now rebuilt?

Questions

Wigton, Whitehaven and Workington

1. **A fountain**. It was erected in 1872 by George Moore in memory of his wife.

2. **St. Mary's.** The Rev Ford redecorated the interior. John Betjeman described it as "a triumph in paint"!

3. **The John Peel Theatre**. It is housed in the old Salvation Army Barracks.

4. **George Washington.** Mildred, his widowed mother, married George Gale in 1700. She died in pregnancy the following year.

5. **True.** The town prospered in the 18th century from tobacco and coal. The Lowther family built the streets in a grid pattern.

6. **The Beacon.** It tells the story of the area's maritime and industrial history.

7. **Sunderland or Tynemouth.** An alternative starting point is Whitehaven.

8. It is a political term, adopted in the 2019 election campaign, describing **a swing voter** of the type found in Workington at the time.

9. **Mary Queen of Scots.** She sheltered at Workington Hall.

10. **Navvies Bridge.** It was originally a railway bridge.

Answers

Eskdale and Borrowdale

1. Which Lake District pass connects Eskdale and Borrowdale?

2. Eskdale Water Mill, near Boot, is a restored working mill. What was it used for?

3. What is the name of the 60ft waterfall not far from Dalegarth Hall?

4. The Eskdale and Ravenglass Steam Railway was built as a tourist attraction. True or False?

5. Eskdale has no lake of its own, but has plenty of tarns. How many can you name?

6. Which woodland in Eskdale Green is home to a Japanese garden?

7. How does the geology of Borrowdale and Eskdale differ from the rest of Cumbria?

8. Which material, commonly associated with pencils, was discovered near Seathwaite in the 16th century?

9. As the crow flies, Seathwaite and Wasdale Head are just under 6km apart, yet the shortest drive between them takes 1hr 30 mins! What's the problem?

10. What name is given to the pass in Borrowdale where the valley narrows.

Questions

Eskdale and Borrowdale

1. **Esk Hause.** The paths from Eskdale, Borrowdale, Wasdale and Langdale meet on Esk Hause.

2. **Grinding corn.** It dates from the16th Century.

3. **Stanley Gyll Force.** It is named after the family who lived at Dalegarth Hall.

4. **False.** It was built to carry iron ore in 1873. Today La'al Ratty carries tourists from Ravenglass to Boot.

5. Burnmoor Tarn, Blea Tarn, Siney Tarn, Blind Tarn, Eel Tarn, Stony Tarn, Muncaster Tarn, Lower Birker Tarn, Foxes Tarn, Broadcrag Tarn and, arguably, Devoke Water.

6. **Giggle Alley.** The garden was created in 1913 but fell into disrepair. The forestry commission is working to restore it.

7. The bedrock of Borrowdale and Eskdale is composed of **volcanic rocks** rather than sedimentary rocks.

8. **Graphite.** It was originally used to mark sheep.

9. **The Langdales are in between.** There are no roads over England's highest mountain range.

10. **The Jaws of Borrowdale** – a place where the steep crags of Grange Fell and Castle Crag meet to form a narrow gap.

Answers

Grasmere and Rydal

1. For what reason is the Dove and Olive, an old Grasmere pub, best remembered?

2. What is the name of the rocky place on the Ambleside road just before Grasmere comes into view?

3. Rydal into Grasmere or Grasmere into Rydal? Which lake drains into which?

4. Which pass to the north of Grasmere, flanked by Helvellyn, is the border between South Lakeland and Allerdale?

5. Rydal Caves on Loughrigg Fell are man-made. True or False?

6. What is the name of the century-old bookshop in Grasmere?

7. Grasmere is famous for sweet things. Gingerbread is one of them. Another is chocolate from an award-winning shop. What is its name?

8. A poet's son, estranged from his father, spent his last years at Nab Cottage, Rydal. Who was he?

9. An historian, who has a museum named after her in Ambleside, lived in Rydal and wrote a history of Grasmere Church. What was her name?

10. You might describe this place in Rydal Hall gardens as 'grotty'. Why is it worth a visit?

Questions

Grasmere and Rydal

1. **It was converted into Dove Cottage**, William Wordsworth's home for eight years from 1799.

2. **Penny Rock.** A penny was added to the rates in the 1830s to pay for the rock blasting needed to build a new turnpike road.

3. **Grasmere into Rydal**.

4. **Dunmail Raise.** It is the only low-level pass connecting north and south Cumbria.

5. **True.** The caves are the remains of an abandoned 19th century slate quarry.

6. **Sam Read.** Sam opened a bookshop in Church Stile in 1887 then moved to Broadgate House in 1895. The business continues there today.

7. **The Chocolate Cottage.** The family-owned shop produces 4,000 handmade chocolates a week.

8. **Hartley Coleridge.** He died an alcoholic there in 1849.

9. **Mary Armitt.** She and her sister lived at Rydal Cottage next to Rydal Church

10. **'The Grot'** is a summerhouse built in the 17th century to view the waterfall nearby.

Answers

Handstand Press

Handstand Press was founded in 2005 from The Tinners' Rabbit Bookshop in Ulverston. It celebrates the history, culture and landscape of Cumbria in publications ranging in content from fiction and poetry, to Cumbria's industrial past, its historic houses and towns and extraordinary landscape.

 If you have enjoyed this quiz and would like to read more about Cumbria and the books we publish go to our website, www.handstandpress.net, for further information. Handstand Press books are available to order from our website, from any good bookshop or on-line.

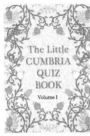

This Place I Know

Handstand Press

This contemporary collection brings the great tradition of Lake District poetry into the 21st Century in a special anthology celebrating the effect of the Cumbrian landscape and people on the imagination.

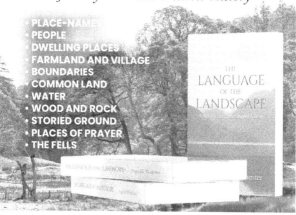

Lightning Source UK Ltd.
Milton Keynes UK
UKHW021954021221
394996UK00005B/275